Crafts to the Rescue

With ideas that save the day

STANDARD PUBLISHING™

CONTENTS

Publisher: Mark Taylor

Director, VBS: Kay Moll

Artist: Dan Foote

Cover Design: Liz Howe Design

Creator: Deonna Lierman

Editor: Karen Roth

Technical Assistance: Dina Sorn

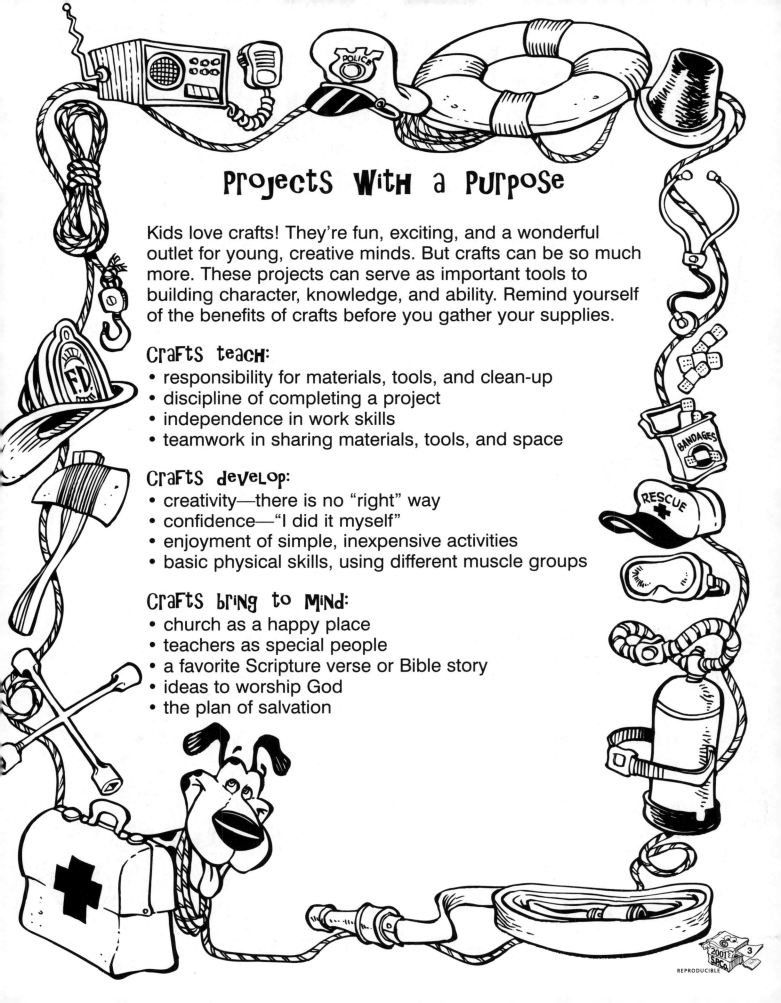

Projects With a Purpose

Kids love crafts! They're fun, exciting, and a wonderful outlet for young, creative minds. But crafts can be so much more. These projects can serve as important tools to building character, knowledge, and ability. Remind yourself of the benefits of crafts before you gather your supplies.

Crafts teach:
- responsibility for materials, tools, and clean-up
- discipline of completing a project
- independence in work skills
- teamwork in sharing materials, tools, and space

Crafts develop:
- creativity—there is no "right" way
- confidence—"I did it myself"
- enjoyment of simple, inexpensive activities
- basic physical skills, using different muscle groups

Crafts bring to mind:
- church as a happy place
- teachers as special people
- a favorite Scripture verse or Bible story
- ideas to worship God
- the plan of salvation

3

HELPFUL HINTS

Make up samples of projects ahead of time to help you know what you need for the project, to give students a visual aid, and to help you anticipate any problems they might encounter.

Remember that these are children's projects, done by children—they shouldn't look like an adult did all the work.

Always use safety equipment.

Choose projects that are appropriate for the students' age level and ability.

When using a photocopier to reproduce pictures with art or type on the back of the page, put black construction paper behind the original.

If you can't make photocopies, use carbon paper for tracing. If it is not available, rub carbon from a pencil onto the back of a design, turn the design over, and trace it onto the desired material.

Have clean-up materials handy before you need them.

Take the time to put down newspapers or plastic coverings to protect the work area. (Old shower curtains work well.)

Paint shirts can be made by cutting holes in the bottoms and sides of plastic garbage bags.

Acrylic paints can be removed from clothing if still wet, but they're permanent when dry. Use denatured alcohol to help remove the pigment from fabric before the paint dries.

When working with small children, provide paste or glue sticks, or dilute glue with a small amount of water. Place the glue in shallow containers on a protected surface. Apply the glue to the paper with old paintbrushes.

PRESCHOOL / KINDERGARTEN

PRESCHOOLERS
- can't sit still for very long
- learn by doing and by repetition
- learn by touching, tasting, smelling, seeing, and hearing
- are learning to share, help, and take turns
- have not mastered scissors, coloring in lines, and folding on lines

KINDERGARTNERS
- like a variety of methods and materials
- can use scissors, glue, large crayons, and large paintbrushes
- enjoy laughing and giggling and may be mischievous
- like to ask "Why?" and want to have reasons for what they are doing
- seek approval from adults for their behavior and their craft projects

SO THEREFORE . . .
- Remember that the process is more important than the finished product.
- Choose appropriate projects that the student (not the teacher) can finish.
- Be prepared with coverings and cleanup materials—some messiness is inevitable.
- Share the love of Jesus in your attitude, your voice, and your actions.

PAPER PLATE FIRE HAT

YOU NEED:
- paper plate
- crayons
- blunt scissors
- tacky-type glue

YOU DO:
Before class begins, cut the plate as shown. Copy badge artwork.

1. Color the fire hat.
2. Color the badge and cut it out.
3. Glue badge to hat as shown.
4. Fold the inside of plate up to make front of hat.

APPLY IT:
As kids wear their hats to and from VBS, they will serve as reminders of the way Jesus can rescue them.

ANIMAL CRACKER ARK

MATERIALS:

CARDBOARD OR CONSTRUCTION PAPER · GLUE · SANDPAPER · SCISSORS · CRAYONS OR MARKERS · ANIMAL CRACKERS

INSTRUCTIONS:

Before class, cut the sandpaper into shapes as shown below. These pieces will become the plank and the roof. Copy the picture of the ark.

1. Color picture with crayons.
2. Glue picture onto cardboard or construction paper.
3. Glue sandpaper plank and roof onto the picture.
4. Glue animal crackers onto the picture.

APPLY IT:

Explain to students that God cares for them just as He cared for Noah and the animals.

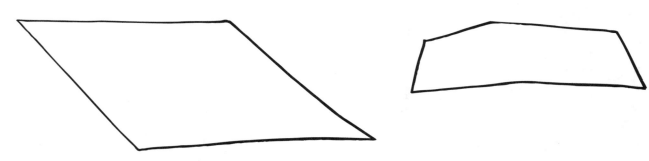

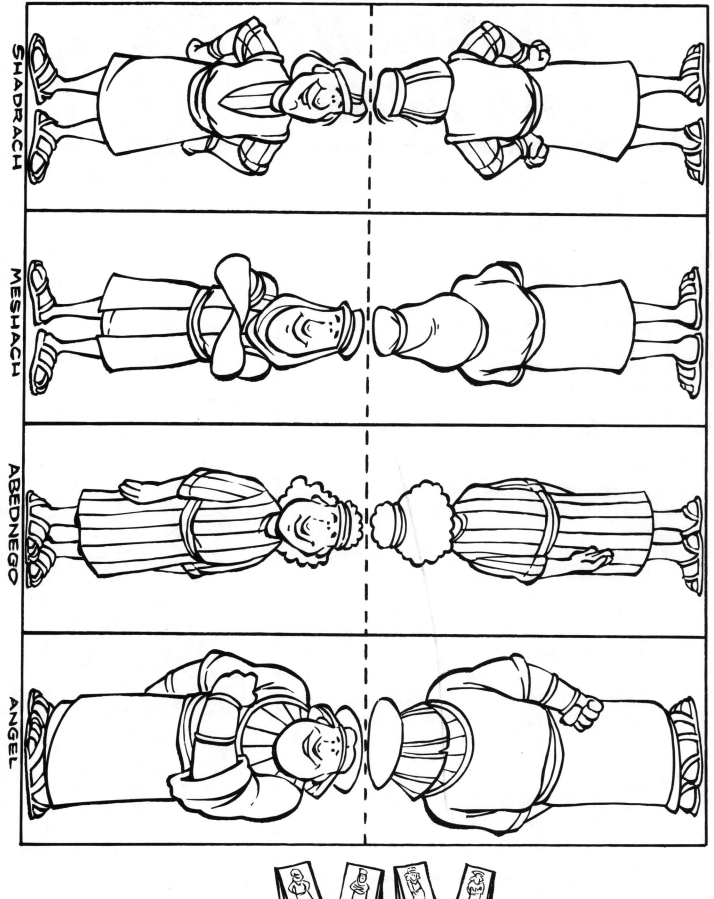

SHADRACH

MESHACH

ABEDNEGO

ANGEL

11

HANDPRINT HANGING

YOU NEED:
- felt pieces (size of your choice)
- tacky-type glue
- stickers, buttons, etc.
- tempera paint
- paint shirt
- water and clean-up materials
- permanent marker
- shallow pan or cookie sheet
- hole punch
- yarn
- small sponge

YOU DO:
Before class, letter "Jesus to the Rescue" on each banner. Punch holes and attach yarn for hanger.

1. Pour paint in a shallow pan. (Be careful not to use too much!)
2. Decorate border of banner with buttons, stickers, etc. Leave the center empty.
3. Use the sponge to dab paint onto child's hand; then carefully press his hand onto the center of the felt. Allow to dry.
   (Optional: Trace child's handprint on construction paper and cut out; then glue onto banner.)

APPLY IT:
This project will help kids remember that God's hand is always there to protect and guide them.

EVER READY MASK

YOU NEED:
- black felt (for ears and nose)
- glue stick
- blunt scissors
- construction paper
- tongue depressor

YOU DO:
Before class, copy picture and mount to construction paper. Cut out holes for eyes and nose piece. Fold nose forward as shown. Using the picture as a guide, make felt pieces for ears and nose.

1. If children are able, allow them to cut out the mask, ears, and nose pieces.
2. Glue the felt pieces onto the mask.
3. Glue tongue depressor to bottom of face area. Enjoy!

APPLY IT:
Explain that puppies are always eager to do what we ask. Tell students that they should always be eager to make God happy by helping others. Let them talk about ways they can serve.

Ever Ready To Serve

PAPER PLATE WALL HANGING

YOU NEED:
- yarn
- tacky-type glue
- blunt scissors
- crayons
- grains, cereals, and bird seeds
- hole punch
- paper plate

YOU DO:
Before class, copy the picture. Cut it out, or allow children to do so themselves.

1. Color the picture.
2. Glue it to the center of the plate.
3. Punch a hole at the top of the plate and make a hanger using a colorful piece of yarn.
4. Allow the children to choose grains, cereals, or seeds and glue them around the plate.

APPLY IT:
God always takes care of our needs. Thank God for His love and care.

PRIMARY/MIDDLER

RESCUE HEB. 13:5

PRIMARIES

- need to know they are loved and supported by the teacher
- enjoy the freedom of working independently
- are happiest when participating in a purposeful activity (in which they know the "hows" and "whys")
- need honest praise, encouragement, and opportunities for success
- want challenging craft activities, but have not yet developed fine-muscle coordination

MIDDLERS

- are developing physically at a steady but slow pace
- are curious explorers, and want to know why they are doing something
- want to be allowed to express themselves
- are searching for self-identity, but still respond to gentle guidance and encouragement from adults

SO THEREFORE . . .

- Show a finished sample of the activity or project. Explain thoroughly so students know the "whys" and "hows".
- Give help as needed, but allow as much self-expression as possible.
- Be prepared for some good-natured rowdiness.
- Provide clean-up materials and have the students clean up on their own as much as possible.
- Have other activities or projects planned for those who finish quickly. This helps to allay any possible discipline problems ahead of time.

RESCUE SHIRTS

YOU NEED:

- newspaper
- craft paper (butcher paper, box paper, etc.)
- glue
- felt pens
- stapler
- scissors

YOU DO:

1. Fold newspaper as shown and cut pattern to appropriate size.
2. Trace pattern onto craft paper.
3. Color or decorate as desired. Add pockets, tie, etc.
4. Copy and color badge of your choice. Cut out badge.
5. Glue badge to the shirt.
6. Staple or glue sides closed.

APPLY IT:

Use these shirts as reminders of a special time of fun and fellowship as kids learn together that Jesus is always near.

HATS OFF TO JESUS

YOU NEED:

two boxes (one approximately 5" x 8"; one approximately 4" x 5"), tape, glue, craft paper (butcher paper, box paper, etc.), cardboard, two plastic caps (from milk or orange juice container), paint, brushes, baseball cap

1 Glue small box on top of larger one and reinforce with tape. Place over a baseball cap and secure with tape.

2 Cover with craft paper. Copy, color, and cut out artwork from the following page. Glue the art onto the boxes. Glue caps to top box as shown.

3 Paint with bright colors.

APPLY IT:

Wear this fun hat as a witness statement: "Hats off to Jesus!"

HATS OFF TO

Jesus

Hebrews 13:5

TIC-TAC-TOE & DOUGH

YOU NEED:
- ingredients for dough (see recipe below)
- glue
- cardboard or corrugation
- scissors
- paint and brushes or felt markers
- ballpoint pen
- small, blunt stick
- (optional) clear adhesive paper, small pebbles and rocks

YOU DO:
1. Copy game board and mount on heavy cardboard or corrugation.
2. Decorate as desired. (Optional: Cover with clear adhesive paper to protect the design.)
3. Glue small pebbles to board if desired.
4. Make dough (see recipe below). Create game pieces by placing flame or bull patterns on dough and tracing art with ballpoint pen. Go over the outline with a small, blunt stick. Allow to dry overnight; then paint.

If you do not wish to make bread dough game pieces, use decorated rocks.

APPLY IT:

This game board provides an excellent way to remember not only the story of Elijah, but the truth that God is greater than anyone or anything in the world. It is also a fine witness tool.

Recipe

YOU NEED:
- 3/4 cup flour
- ½ cup salt
- 1½ t. alum
- 1½ t. vegetable oil
- ½ cup boiling water
- food coloring
- pan
- bowl
- spoon
- airtight container

YOU DO:
1. Combine flour, salt, and alum in bowl.
2. Boil water in pan, add oil, and add to mixture in bowl. Stir.
3. Add food coloring and knead until blended. Makes one cup.
4. Store in airtight container until ready to use. Dries hard overnight.

GREATER IS HE THAT IS IN YOU THAN HE THAT IS IN THE WORLD.

1 JOHN 4:4

FIREBALL CANDY CADDIE

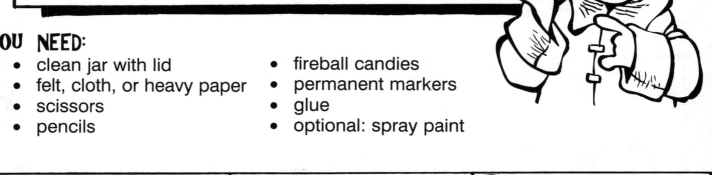

YOU NEED:

- clean jar with lid
- felt, cloth, or heavy paper
- scissors
- pencils
- fireball candies
- permanent markers
- glue
- optional: spray paint

① (Optional: Spray paint the jar lid.)

② Copy patterns and trace them onto felt, cloth, or heavy paper. Color patterns as desired.

③ Glue patterns onto jar. Fill with fireball candies.

APPLY IT:

This project is a great reminder of the story of Shadrach, Meshach, and Abednego and the importance of fireproof faith. Kids will remember that God is with them, even in times of trouble.

Fire-Proof Faith

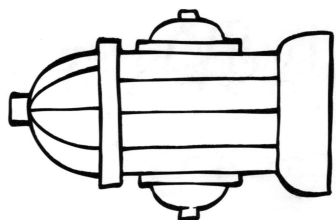

CREATE-A-CROSS

YOU NEED:

- 10 1/2" x 8" piece of cardboard for backing of cross
- wooden stick matches
- glue
- brown acrylic paint
- paintbrushes
- permanent markers
- scissors
- pop can tab

①
Before class burn approximately 100 matches (adults only). Allow to cool.

②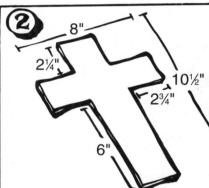
8"
2¼"
10½"
2¾"
6"
Cut cross out of cardboard. (See illustration.) Paint background brown. Paint edges/sides also.

③
Glue matches to cross as shown.

④
Copy the "Jesus Gives Life" pattern. Color as desired and glue onto cross.

⑤
Glue remaining matches as shown. Then glue a pop can tab to back of the cross for use as a hanger.

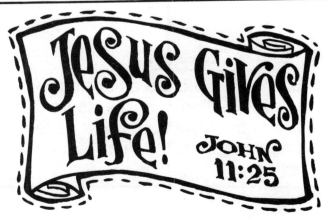
Jesus Gives Life! John 11:25

APPLY IT:
This powerful symbol is a constant reminder that Jesus gives life.

23

WALLPAPER BIBLE COVER

①

YOU NEED:
- scrap wallpaper
- Bible
- scissors
- pencil

②

YOU DO:
Lay wallpaper out. Open Bible and place in center of wallpaper. Cut paper 3-4" larger (on all sides) than the Bible.

③

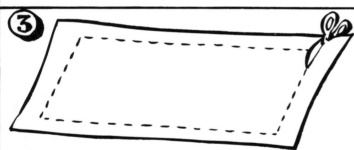

Mark around edges of Bible. Allow an additional 2" border around the edge marks and cut out paper.

④

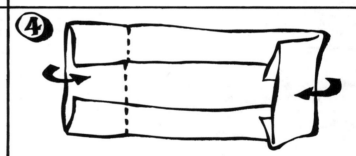

Fold as shown.

⑤

Insert Bible and decorate as desired. Add "Heed What You Read" design to front cover. *It may be easier to make a pattern first, using newsprint. Then use it to cut your final cover.*

APPLY IT:
Read Philippians 4:19 with your students. Remind them that God's Word has the answers to rescue us from all of life's struggles.

FIND-A-FRIEND BOOKMATES

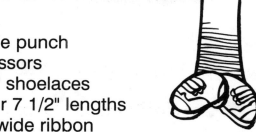

YOU NEED:

- copy of Bookmate heads and feet
- poster board
- glue or rubber cement
- markers or colored pencils
- hole punch
- scissors
- 12" shoelaces
- four 7 1/2" lengths of wide ribbon

YOU DO:

1. Color the heads and feet of the Bookmates as desired. Mount them on poster board and cut them out.
2. Punch two holes through each pair of feet. Thread a shoelace through the holes in each pair of feet and tie into a bow.
3. Glue a head and a pair of feet to the ends of a ribbon.

APPLY IT:

Tell students to give Bookmates to their friends, and ask God to use them as rescuers in the lives of those people.

PENCIL PAL

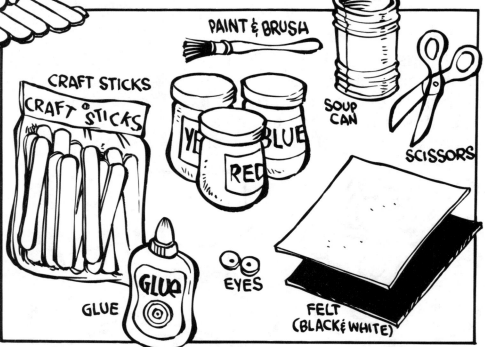

PAINT & BRUSH

CRAFT STICKS

CRAFT STICKS

YELLOW BLUE

RED

SOUP CAN

SCISSORS

GLUE

EYES

FELT (BLACK & WHITE)

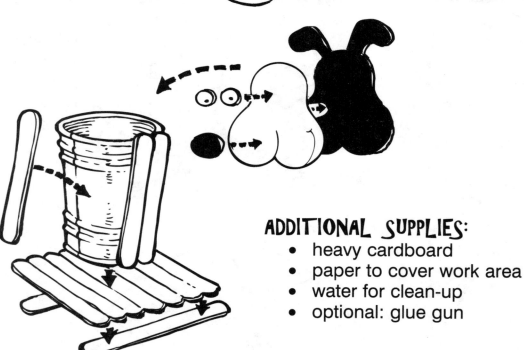

ADDITIONAL SUPPLIES:
- heavy cardboard
- paper to cover work area
- water for clean-up
- optional: glue gun

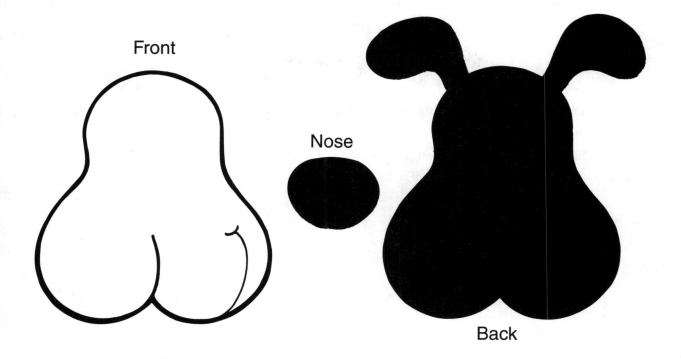

Front

Nose

Back

YOU DO:

1. Determine how many craft sticks you'll need to surround the can and to create a platform. Do this by placing the craft sticks edge-to-edge around the can and beneath it.
2. Paint the desired number of sticks. Be sure to paint the front, sides and back of each stick using a variety of bright colors. Allow to dry.
3. Copy and cut out patterns for dog. (See illustration.) Use the patterns to cut the back section out of black felt and the front section from white felt.
4. Glue white felt to cardboard (for the face) and trim edges. Glue black felt to the back of the cardboard (to make the ears).
5. Glue eyes and nose to face. Allow to dry.
6. Glue platform together as shown and glue the can to platform.
7. Glue sticks around can.
8. Glue face piece to craft sticks.

APPLY IT:

This Pencil Pal will remind kids to be ever-ready to serve God.

FIREPROOF FAITH DECOUPAGE WALL ART

YOU NEED:

- wood for plaque
- copy of art (sized to fit wood)
- colored pencils or permanent markers
- scissors
- glue
- sandpaper
- shellac
- matches (for adult use only)
- wall hanger
- (optional: full color artwork of your choice in place of the one provided, paint and brushes)

YOU DO:

Before class an adult should carefully burn the edges of the art to give it an antiqued look.

1. Paint the wood plaque (optional).
2. Color the picture as desired and cut out.
3. Center the artwork on the plaque and glue in place.
4. When the glue is completely dry, spray or paint the picture with shellac and let dry overnight. You may wish to sand the picture lightly and apply a second coat of shellac and let dry a second night (if time allows).
5. Add a hanger to the center back of the project.

APPLY IT:

Sometimes faith seems hard, but a fireproof faith is one that will last no matter what problems may come. Explain to students that God has said that He will never leave or forsake them (Hebrews 13:5).

5TH-6TH/TEEN

5TH AND 6TH GRADERS

- are beginning their growth spurts, and consequently will suffer mood swings
- love competition, but often lack confidence in their abilities
- are strongly motivated by peer pressure and are looking for heroes to imitate
- appreciate some attention, but are uncomfortable with outwardly emotional displays of affection or attention

TEENS

- are growing rapidly and becoming more sexually aware
- are developing their own self-concepts and need to be accepted for who they are
- put up fronts sometimes and can be outwardly cruel to each other
- need significant Christian adult examples who are not afraid to confront them if needed

SO THEREFORE . . .

- Provide projects that will sufficiently challenge the students, but will be fun too.
- Plan adequately—for the project itself, and for those students who finish quickly.
- Provide opportunities for fellowship and sharing together during craft time.
- Be an example of Christian love—because it may be a real challenge! Don't take literally everything a young teen says. Don't be afraid to confront or talk with students; they can spot a counterfeit a mile away.

POCKET PLACEMATS

YOU NEED:
- old shirt (pocket T or button-front)
- thin corrugation (approximately 14" x 18")
- scissors or pinking shears
- chalk
- iron
- fusible web (found at fabric stores)
- badge patterns on page 17
- carbon paper
- pencil
- fabric paints

YOU DO:
1. Cut a 14" x 18" rectangle from corrugation to use as a template.
2. Smooth out shirt and place template over the top of the shirt. (Be sure to include the pocket.)
3. Trace outline of template with chalk and remove template. Carefully cut along lines, through front and back of the shirt.
4. Fold in raw edges of shirt, and then iron (adults only).
5. Use fusible web to secure the edges of fabric together.
6. (Optional: To make a permanent seam, use a sewing machine to finish the edges.)
7. Use carbon paper to transfer badge design (or create your own). Decorate with fabric paints.

APPLY IT:
Let students use these place mats as a daily reminder to thank God for His constant care.

5/6-Teen

RESCUE BOOKENDS

YOU NEED:

- six pieces of wood, 1/4" -1/2" thick: two pieces 5" x 5 3/8" (for ark); two pieces 5" x 5" for base (bottom pieces); two pieces 5" x 6" for upright back piece
- carbon paper
- scroll saw
- acrylic paint
- paintbrushes
- clear acrylic spray (optional)
- red ballpoint pen
- permanent markers (fine point, black or brown)
- sandpaper
- brown stain or shoe polish
- glue

YOU DO:

Before class, trace the ark pattern onto both sides of the wood pieces, using the transfer paper and pen. Outline with permanent marker. Cut out ark shape with a saw.

1. Sand all edges of wood.
2. Paint as desired and allow to dry.
3. Stain wood with shoe polish or wood stain and allow to dry.
4. Assemble bookends as shown in illustration above: glue the 5" x 5" bases to the 5" x 6" backs to form an "L" shape. Center the ark pieces on the base pieces and glue in position. Allow to dry.
5. Cut out words from the pattern and glue to base and back pieces as shown in illustration. When dry, apply a second coat of glue as a sealer and allow to dry completely.
6. (Optional: Spray with a clear coat of acrylic to give it a shine.)

APPLY IT:

Students can use these bookends as a visual reminder that God is always there to help—even when life is hectic.

ZOO

When Life's a Rescues you!

GOD

© 2001 SPCo

33

5/6-Teen

FUN FEEDER

YOU NEED:
- 8" x 10" piece of wood or heavy plastic (3/8" - 1/2" thick)
- drill
- scroll saw
- acrylic paint
- paintbrushes
- cord
- carbon paper
- red ballpoint pen
- plastic lid to hold birdseed
- hole punch
- permanent marker
- sandpaper
- birdseed

YOU DO:
Before class, copy and transfer both patterns (at desired size) to wood or heavy plastic using carbon paper and red pen. Cut out pieces and drill holes in sign and hands as indicated.

1. Sand rough edges on wood; trace over design using permanent marker
2. Paint as desired. Use the permanent marker to reestablish lines that may have been lost during painting.
3. Punch or drill four holes in plastic lid
4. Using cord, assemble as shown.

APPLY IT:
Just as this project will help to care for God's creatures, it will remind students that He promises to take care of them (Philippians 4:19).

5/6-Teen

EVER READY TOWEL HOLDER

YOU NEED:

- 7 1/2" x 22" piece of wood, 3/4" thick; divide into three sections—**base** (7 1/2" x 8"), **dog** (7 1/2" x 10"), and **muzzle** (7 1/2" x 4")
- dowel rod (3/4" x 11")
- saw
- wood glue
- drill
- acrylic paint
- paintbrush
- carbon paper
- red ballpoint pen
- sandpaper
- permanent marker
- (optional) brown shoe polish

① Transfer the dog and muzzle designs onto the wood using carbon paper and pen. Cut out the base, the dog, and muzzle pieces. Sand all wood edges. Using a permanent marker, trace over the outline of the dog.

② Glue the dog to one of the short sides of the base. Drill a 3/4" hole in the center of the base. Insert the dowel into the center hole; glue and allow to dry. Glue the muzzle to the face of the dog. Allow to dry.

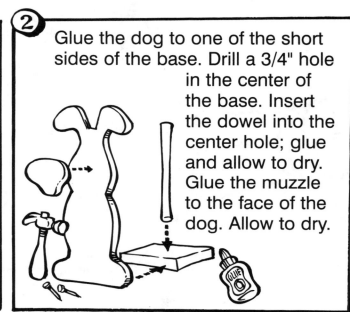

③ Paint the dog as desired. Stain the base with brown shoe polish if you wish, or simply paint it.

APPLY IT: Students should use this towel holder as a reminder to be ever ready to serve God.

5/6-Teen

37

REPRODUCIBLE

FLOWER-POT PUPPY

YOU NEED:

- four small pots (for legs)
- one larger pot (for body)
- bead chain (must fit around large pot)
- large colored bead with hole
- black felt
- white spray paint
- black acrylic paint
- paintbrushes
- red permanent marker
- pair of movable eyes
- white glue
- hot glue gun (for adult use only)
- cardboard
- scissors
- plastic hat
- small sponge
- cotton ball

YOU DO:

1. Paint all pots white and allow to dry.
2. Using a small sponge, dab black spots on the pots. Draw toes on paws (see illustration above).
3. Use the pattern to cut ears out of black felt, and then glue ears to top of large pot.
4. Copy the face pattern to desired size; then cut it out. Color the tongue red, and glue to front of large pot. Add eyes to face.

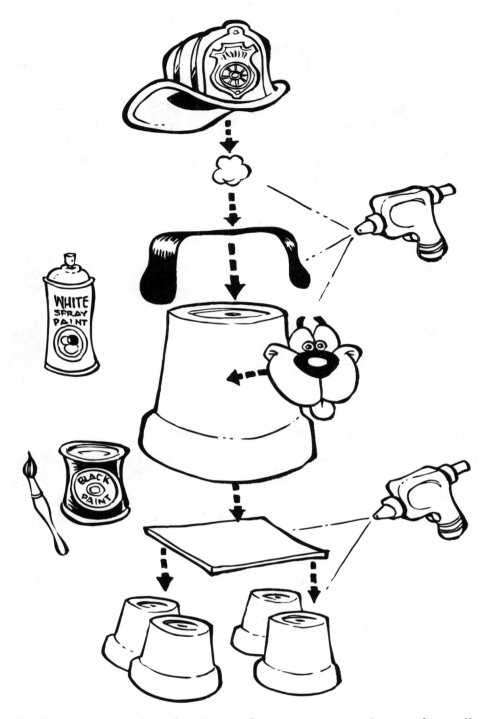

5. Group small pots together for legs. Cut a square piece of cardboard just large enough to cover all four legs together. (This piece will hold the legs in place and support the large pot.) Hot glue cardboard in place.
6. Place the large pot on top of the cardboard and secure with hot glue.
7. Thread the bead chain through the bead and clasp shut. Paint as desired. Secure bead chain around the large pot for dog collar and tags.
8. Glue cotton ball to top of large pot (over ears). Glue hat in place.

APPLY IT:

Dogs are very faithful. Students can use this flowerpot puppy as a constant reminder to be faithful to God in everything they say and do.

JESUS IS A "MAZE"ING GAME

YOU NEED:
- shoe box
- plastic drinking straws
- toy marble
- scissors
- paper (white or colored) to cover shoe box
- white glue
- crayons or felt markers

YOU DO:
1. Cover shoe box with paper and glue in place.
2. Cut straws to create a maze (see illustration) and glue in place.
3. Copy, color, and cut out art to decorate sides of box.
4. Glue art in place as desired.
5. Mark start and finish points in the maze; then drop in a marble and play!

APPLY IT:
Life sometimes seems like a maze, with twists and turns that are pretty confusing. Explain to students that Jesus and His a"maze"ing love are always right there to see them through to the finish!

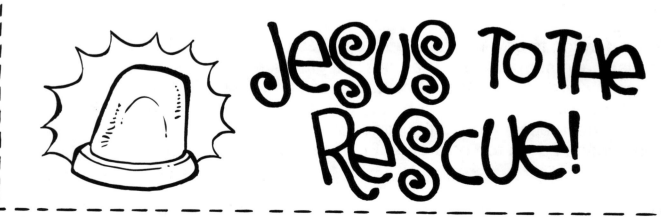

JESUS TO THE RESCUE!

JESUS IS

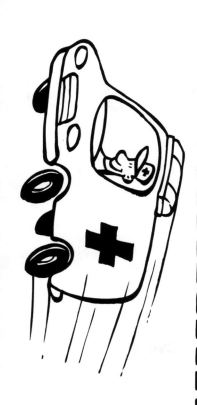

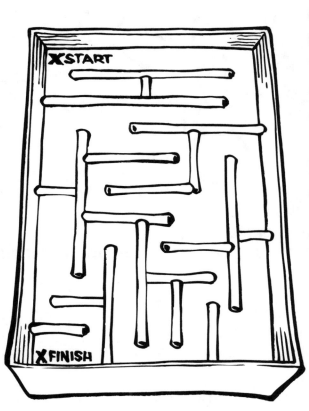

X START

X FINISH

A"MAZE"ING!

5/6-Teen

EZ IRON-ONS

YOU NEED:
- computer, scanner, and printer
- iron-on paper (found at computer or office-supply stores)
- iron
- scissors
- fabric paints
- brushes

YOU DO:
1. Scan the art on the following page. Reduce or enlarge the art if you wish. Flop the art on your computer screen, so that it appears backwards.
2. Print the design on special iron-on paper.
3. Cut out the images and transfer them to clothes. (Use the manufacturer's recommendations for transferring.)
4. Use fabric paints to paint your project. Allow the paint to dry completely.
5. Let paint dry for at least 72 hours before washing. Turn the item inside-out before putting it in the washing machine.

APPLY IT:
These iron-ons will be fun witness tools as students become rescuers for Jesus.

FLEA SATAN

1 JOHN 4:4

Jesus

HITS THE SPOT

43

TIN PUNCH "CAN"DLE HOLDER

YOU NEED:

- clean soup can (remove label)
- small candle
- round log (end must fit inside can)
- small nail
- small hammer
- tape

Copy artwork below or create your own design; cut it out and tape to the can.

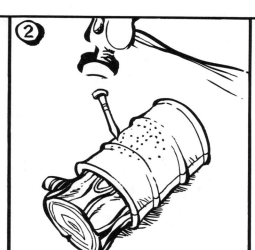

Insert the end of log in can. Using a hammer and nail, punch the design into the can.

Remove log and paper pattern. Place candle inside can.

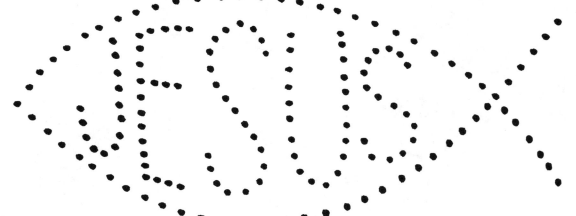

APPLY IT:

Jesus is the light of the world, and He is able to rescue us from the darkness of sin. Read 1 John 1:9 together and discuss its meaning.

BUCKET SHOWER

YOU NEED:

- clean plastic bucket with handle
- small drill (for adult use only)
- utility knife (for adult use only)
- two plastic foam tubes (pool toys)
- warm or cold glue gun
- permanent marker
- paints and brushes
- water
- carbon paper
- ballpoint pen

YOU DO:

1. Copy and enlarge art for face.
2. Drill small holes all the way around the bucket, about 1" apart and 3/4" from the bottom.
3. Transfer face to bucket with transfer paper. Trace over the lines with a permanent marker. Add spots and paint as desired.
4. Cut the foam tubes in smaller pieces and glue legs around the bucket as shown. Allow to dry thoroughly.

APPLY IT:

Kids can hang the bucket from a pole or tree limb, add water, and enjoy some fun. Remind them that Jesus gives us all we need, showering us with blessings every day. Don't forget to thank Him!

FLOWERPOT FIREMAN

YOU NEED:
- clay pot
- permanent marker
- movable eyes
- acrylic paint
- paintbrush
- moss
- pair of curly shoelaces
- two small plastic cups
- plastic hat
- tacky-type glue or hot glue gun
- scissors
- black spray paint

YOU DO:

Before class, spray the inside of small plastic cups with black spray paint. Allow to dry.

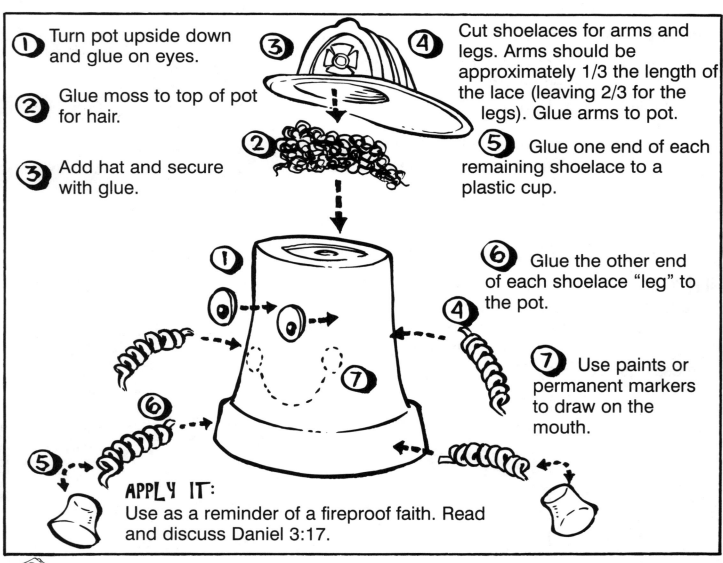

① Turn pot upside down and glue on eyes.

② Glue moss to top of pot for hair.

③ Add hat and secure with glue.

④ Cut shoelaces for arms and legs. Arms should be approximately 1/3 the length of the lace (leaving 2/3 for the legs). Glue arms to pot.

⑤ Glue one end of each remaining shoelace to a plastic cup.

⑥ Glue the other end of each shoelace "leg" to the pot.

⑦ Use paints or permanent markers to draw on the mouth.

APPLY IT:
Use as a reminder of a fireproof faith. Read and discuss Daniel 3:17.

YOU NEED:

- four square boxes (13" or larger)
- scissors
- transparencies
- overhead projector
- glue
- soft-lead pencil
- permanent marker
- paint and brushes

GIANT BLOCK PUZZLE

YOU DO:

1. Photocopy the art and separate the figures. Then photocopy each figure onto a separate transparency.
2. Glue box bottoms and tops closed. (Tape extended onto the sides will prevent a clear picture.)
3. Stack boxes on top of each other to create a tower. Project art (one figure at a time) onto the boxes. Trace the outlines using a soft-lead pencil. Align the dotted line (on the top part of each piece of art) with the bottom of the top box. This will insure proper alignment of each figure.
4. When you are satisfied with the finished tracings, go over the outlines with a permanent marker.
5. Paint each character as desired.

APPLY IT:

This giant puzzle can be used to decorate a room. It can also be used as a game by creating two sets of figures, mixing them up or placing them in one big pile, and having two teams of kids work to stack the boxes in order. The team who finishes first wins.

Talk about how Jesus is able to unscramble our lives and help us put them back in order.

Fun Stuff

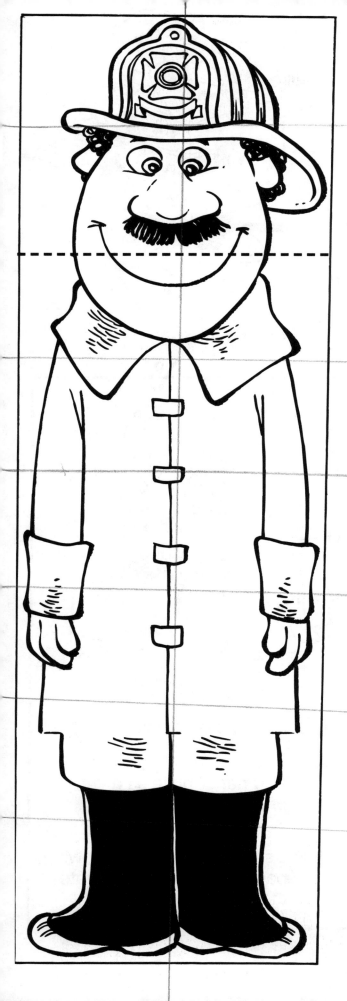

JUST PLANE FUN

YOU NEED:
- cardboard box
- sharp utility knife (for adult use only)
- paper plate (for propeller)
- long paper fasteners
- paint
- paintbrushes
- black permanent marker
- glue gun

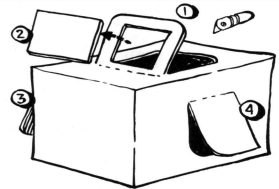

① Using the illustration as a guide, draw and cut out cockpit area.

② Cut out section of windshield. It will be used as the rudder.

③ Cut out sections for wings.

④

⑤ Cut out section for rudder as shown. The circle becomes a cap for the propeller (8).

⑥ Score rudder (tail section).

⑦ Hot glue tail section in place.

⑧ Add paper plate as a propeller.

⑨ Use patterns on the following page to paint and decorate the plane.

ReSCUe

Hebrews 13:5

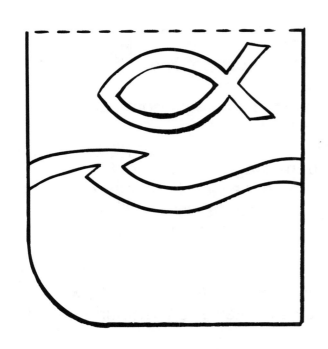

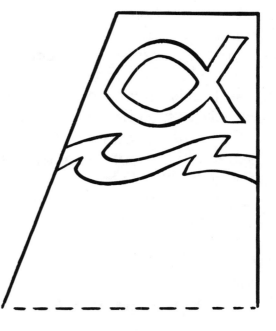

DING-A-LING DOG CHIMES

YOU NEED:
- two clay pots of graduating sizes, according to your choice
- black vinyl (for ears)
- black and white paint (acrylic or exterior latex)
- red acrylic paint
- weatherproof cord
- 1 1/2" x 2 1/2" piece of wood (for clapper)
- hole punch
- drill
- paintbrush
- pencil
- carbon paper
- red ballpoint pen
- two wooden beads
- black permanent marker

YOU DO:
1. Paint pots and their edges with white paint.
2. Turn pots upside down. Draw a face on the larger pot and spots on both pots using a permanent marker or paint.
3. Use the illustration on page 55 as a guide to make ears from black vinyl. Punch a small hole in the center for the cord.
4. Using small beads and knots to hold the pots and beads in place, assemble the pots as shown, adjusting the length as desired.
5. Trace the "Jesus to the Rescue" pattern onto the wood with carbon paper and a pen. Outline with permanent marker. Paint as desired.
6. Drill a hole in the clapper and attach to the end of the cord as shown.

APPLY IT:
Students can use this project as a constant reminder that Jesus is always with them. It will also serve as a prominent witness statement when hung outside.

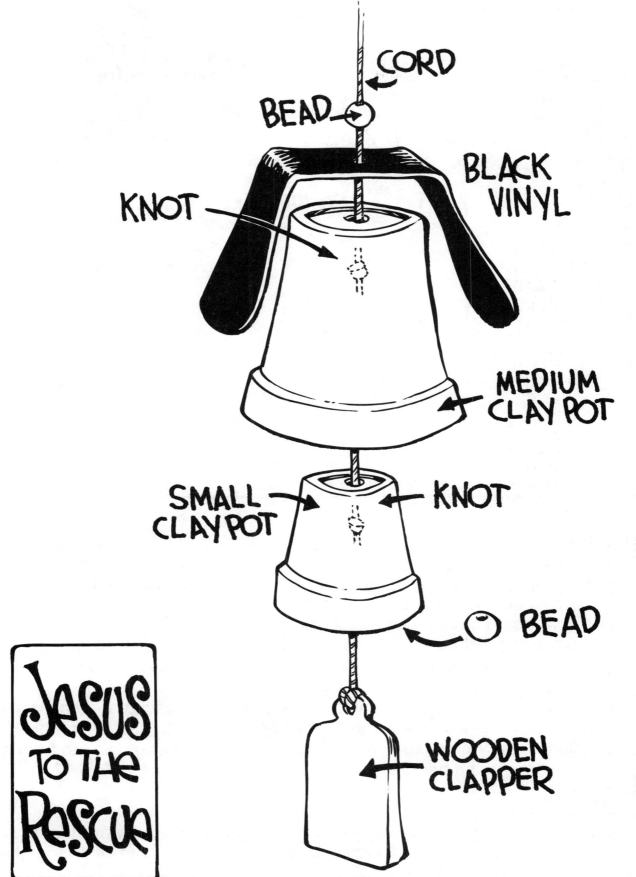

CORD

BEAD

KNOT

BLACK VINYL

MEDIUM CLAY POT

SMALL CLAY POT

KNOT

BEAD

WOODEN CLAPPER

Jesus TO THE Rescue

3-D PICTURE PLAQUE

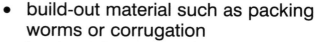

YOU NEED:

- build-out material such as packing worms or corrugation
- boxboard or poster board for backing pictures
- scissors
- white glue
- colored pencils (soft lead works best)
- rubber cement
- cardboard or pop can tab (for hanger)

YOU DO:

1. Copy the picture and build-out pieces to desired size.
2. Dry mount the picture to the backing sheet with rubber cement. Do so by putting rubber cement on both surfaces, letting them dry, and then putting the two pieces together.
3. Trim board so that backing is not larger than picture.
4. Color the picture as desired.
5. Carefully cut out the build-out pieces: two bears, four corner circles, and the word, "God."
6. Glue the build-out material to the large piece of background art; then glue the small art pieces to the build-out material. (See diagram.)
7. To display your picture, make a cardboard easel or glue a tab from a pop can to the back.

APPLY IT:

Explain that, no matter how tough the struggle, God is always there to help His children. Read 2 Corinthians 12:9 and Philippians 4:19 together.

When you can't swim another stroke...

2 Cor. 12:9

Philippians 4:19

...let GOD be your Life preserver!

Philippians 4:19

GOD

2 Cor. 12:9

(build-out pieces)

Fun Stuff

CARDBOARD FIGURES

YOU NEED:
- large sheets of cardboard or a refrigerator box
- glue
- sharp utility knife (for adult use only)
- marker or pen
- paint
- paintbrush
- "rescue" clothes for figures

YOU DO:
1. Trace the outline of a child or adult onto the cardboard.
2. (Adults only) Cut out the cardboard shape.
3. Using the illustrations above, copy art for face, enlarging it to the proper size to fit your cutout.
4. Paint face and hands. Glue face to body.
5. Dress figure in rescue clothes.
6. Use to decorate your VBS, church, home, etc.

APPLY IT:
Hebrews 13:5 tells us that Jesus will never leave us, no matter who we are or what we look like. Remind students that He will always be there for us!

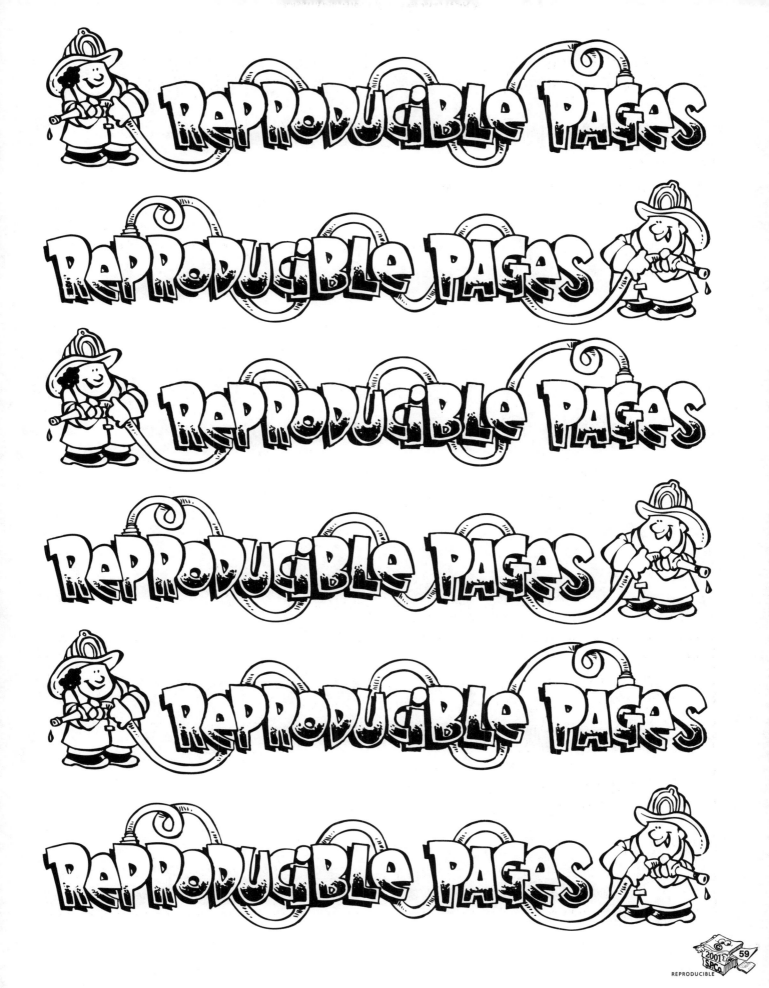

IDEAS FOR USING THESE LETTERS:

- Copy the letters and create posters and bulletin boards.
- Copy the letters and play a game as you try to name objects that start with each letter.
- Copy the letters and use them as the first letter on name tags.
- Trace the letters with permanent markers onto clear acetate and use to decorate windows.

When Life's a Zoo...
God Rescues You!

Ephesians 2:8

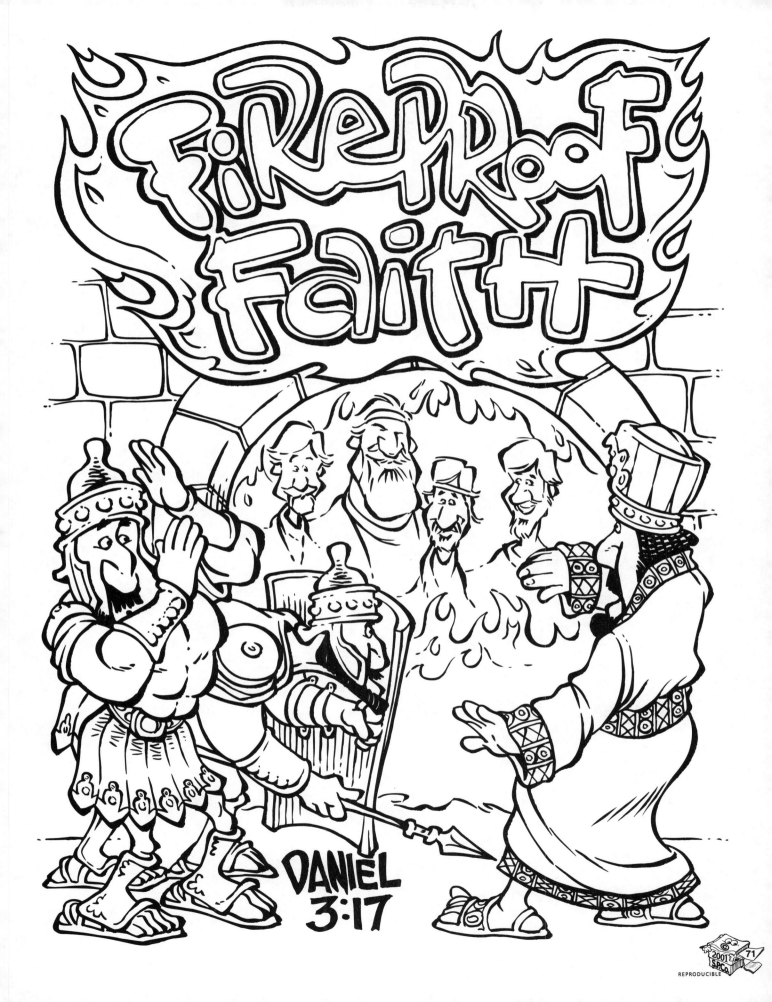

GREATER IS HE

THAT IS IN YOU...

1 JOHN 4:4

THAN HE THAT IS IN THE WORLD!

TRUST IS A MUST

PSALM 56:3

AWARD OF EXCELLENCE

KEEP PLUGGIN' AWAY!

PRESENTED TO:

_____
(Name)

DATE: _____

TEACHER: _____

Outstanding Rescue Member

AWARD

PRESENTED TO:

_____
(Name)

DATE: _____

TEACHER: _____